Preaching the Seven Last Sayings of Jesus Christ on the Cross

by Reverend Dr. Vincent P. Taylor

PublishAmerica
Baltimore

First printing

PublishAmerica has allowed this work to remain exactly as the author intended, verbatim, without editorial input.

Cover Design by:
The Community of Faith Christian Church
www.tcofcc.org
© Copyright 2008

ISBN: 1-60610-051-3
PUBLISHED BY PUBLISHAMERICA, LLLP
www.publishamerica.com
Baltimore

Printed in the United States of America

Table of Contents

The Foreword
Preaching the Seven Last Sayings of Jesus Christ on the Cross

Dr. Vincent Taylor in his book, *Preaching the Seven Last Sayings of Jesus Christ on the Cross*, has afforded preachers and Christians alike a personal journey into the final, complete and redemptive work of Jesus for humanity. Dr. Taylor takes great care in analyzing and projecting the pain and agony of Jesus the Christ as He hung on Calvary's cross. Dr. Taylor takes an audacious step in writing and preaching these seven sayings of Jesus from the Cross. Throughout history preachers have attempted to bring light to this very dark moment in human history. I believe Dr. Taylor has succeeded in giving the reader a closer glimpse into the agony and even beauty of Christ's love for sinful humanity.

Each word is carefully and thoughtfully approached with a beneficial introduction before each sermon that aides the reader in understanding the nuances of biblical scholarship. In fact, it's my opinion that in some cases the introductions bring more light than the actual sermon. This is no slight on the sermons; however, in some cases the introductions gives insight that can only be captured from research and scholarship. While some preachers attempt to romance the text, Dr. Taylor stays clear of this temptation and gives the reader a sincere account of what Good Friday represented. His sermons cause the reader to revisit the Cross in a personal and real manner and come away with a deeper appreciation for the price that was paid by Jesus on the cross. Dr. Taylor has given the Christian community a document which will enrich our personal lives as we embrace the notion of sacrifice and commitment during the Lenten season and beyond. This book will set your heart on fire for the passion of Jesus Christ.

Rev. Dr. William E. Harris Jr.,
Sr. Pastor Believers Christian Fellowship Church
Dayton, Ohio

Prologue

Several of my closest friends; as well as, several of my colleagues have asked, "What led me to write yet another book on the subject of the Seven Last Sayings of Jesus Christ on the Cross?" I must confess that in the beginning the question to some degree bothered me. I was some what disturbed because I completely understand that the majority of people who know me and know me well, recognize that I'm the kind of person who spends time praying; as well as, time in deep thought regarding every decision I make. I simply will not do anything without first considering and weighing the cost and considering all the consequences. The implication of their question is not that the subject isn't worthy of further consideration, explanation or writing, but their point is literally hundreds of books have been written on the subject of the seven last sayings of Jesus Christ on the Cross. But the uniqueness of this book is that it offers something the other books do not. This book shares seven detailed sermons written in the way I believe Jesus would have preached them.

To answer the question I offer four explanations. First God has inspired and instructed me to write this book. Secondly, I've possessed a deep interest in the subject matter for a very long time. Thirdly, the majority of books which I've read on this subject address the seven last sayings of Jesus Christ as simple meditations. Thoughts of the seven last expressions; uttered by our Lord, while suffering and dying on the cross.

At issue for me is the word, meditations. Many I believe would argue the point that all followers of Christianity and Judaism should spend time meditating, thinking and praying over the seven last saying of our Lord. The psalmist declares that a *"blessed man…delights and meditates day and night in the law (Word) of the Lord"* Psalms (1:1-2). *"O how love I thy law! It is my meditation all the day"* (Psalm 119:97). We should meditate, think and pray over the entire Word of God, the complete Bible and not just these last seven expressions of our Lord.

Finally, my reason for writing on this subject stems from

the belief that not only should we mediate, think and pray about these sayings, but we should be bold enough and daring enough to go behind the sayings. If you're familiar with my first my first book entitled, "When a Nobody Becomes Somebody", or if you've attended any conference which I've conducted, you're familiar with the following: in the words of Rev. Dr. H. Beecher Hicks we must remember that there is a word behind the Word, a logos behind the Logos. Theologians refer to this as the revealed or secret word of God. *"The secret things Belong unto the Lord our God: but those things which are revealed belong unto us and to our children for ever, that we may do all the words of this law"* (Deut. 29:29). There's a secret word, a revealed word which the Holy Spirit has shown me about these powerful seven last sayings of Jesus Christ on the Cross. It's my hope and prayer that you will continue to travel with me and read this written work, as we unlock together the secret word.

Dedication

This book is dedicated to my late grandparents, Mr. Noble and Mrs. Geraldine Brooks, Mr. James and Mrs. Sarah Taylor. My life is richer because of you.

In addition Rev. Abraham Brown, Pastor of the First Baptist Church of College Hill, Tampa, Florida. Thank you for touching my life with the gift of humility.

Acknowledgment

Special thanks to Ms. Brenna Fields for your editorial contribution and spiritual support.

Preaching the Seven Last Sayings of Jesus Christ on the Cross

Introduction

A common text book definition for Expository Preaching states that it is the communication of a Biblical concept derived from and transmitted through a historical, grammatical, and literary study of a biblical passage, in its context, which the Holy Spirit first applies to the personality and experience of the preacher, then through the preacher to the hearer. My understanding and comprehension of this definition combined with prayer are the sole means whereby I've attempted to discuss and share these written and preached sermons regarding the seven last sayings of Jesus Christ on the Cross.

Permit me to say openly and honestly that greater, smarter and far more articulate preachers than I have preached on Good Friday these seven last sayings of Jesus Christ. It's my prayer that these sermons will serve as a model for young preachers, particularly those who attend churches which annually observe the age old tradition of preaching the seven last saying of Jesus Christ. I trust this work will live up to the tradition and example of great Preachers; those who have come and gone before me; as well as those who currently, Sunday after Sunday throughout America preach with passion and boldness. Finally, I pray that God has permitted me to capture the essence of Black Preaching, which in my opinion is the ability to examine a biblical text, exegesis the text, contemporize the text and blend the text with rich story telling to produce and deliver not only great writing but sermons which will serve as a paradigm for great preaching.

For Christians, Good Friday is the crucial day, not just during a single year but world history itself. The source of the word crucial is significant. It comes from the Latin *crux*, meaning "cross". Webster's dictionary defines crucial as "having the nature of a final choice of supreme trail; supremely critical; decisive." First century Christians and Apostles, declared the Cross and Resurrection of Jesus

Christ to be the decisive turning point for all the ages of the created universe (Col. 1:15-20; Heb. 1:1-4).

The New Testament Gospels each record at least one of the seven last sayings from the crucified Jesus of Nazareth. It has long been customary on Good Friday to preach seven short sermons on the Seven Last Sayings. In the traditional order, the first saying is from the Gospel of Luke: *"Father, forgive them, for they know not what they do."* The second saying is also found in the Gospel of Luke: *"Truly, I say to you, today you will be with me in paradise."* The third saying is found in the Gospel of John: *"Woman, behold, your son!"* *Then He said to the disciple, "Behold, your mother."* The fourth saying is found in the Gospel of Matthew: *"Eli, Eli, la ma sabach thani?"* *that is "My God, My God, why have you forsaken me?"* The fifth saying is found in the Gospel of John: *"I thirst."* The sixth saying is found in the Gospel of John: *"It is finished."* The seventh saying is found in the Gospel of Luke: *"Father, into thy hands I commend my spirit."*

In Jesus' time, crucifixion was not against the law. It was carried out via the law. It was an exceptionally gruesome manner of torturing a person to death, carried out by the Roman government not in secret, but in public view. Mel Gibson's celebrated film *The Passion of the Christ* does not fully convey the full ghastliness of crucifixion to the modern audience. We do not understand it because we have never seen anything like it. The situation was very different in Jesus' earthly time. It was common place for people to see crucified men along the roadsides of the Roman Empire.

People know what it looked like, smelled like, and sounded like. The horrific sight of completely naked men in agony, the smell and sight of their bodily functions taking place in full view of those that passed by.The sounds of their groans and labored breathing going on for hours and, in some case, for days. All of this took place in public, and no one cared. Perhaps this is why the book of Lamentations earlier recorded the Good Friday scene this way: "*Is it nothing to you, all you who pass by?* (1:12).

Jews and Gentiles perceived crucified persons through the same lenses, as low and despised. Crucifixion sent an unmistakable signal, this person that you see before you is not fit to live, not even human (as the Romans put it, such a person was *damnatio ad bestias*, meaning "condemned to the death of a beast".

Crucifixions were meant to be obscene, in the original sense of the word; the Oxford English Dictionary suggests "disgusting, repulsive, filthy, foul, abominable, and loathsome." It is important to note that in a time when crucifixion was still occurring and was widely practiced throughout the Roman Empire, Christians were proclaiming a degraded, condemned, *crucified* person as the Son of God and Savior of the world.

Much of society is accustomed to seeing crosses, wearing them on chains, carrying them in processions, and so on, that it is almost impossible to grasp their original horror.

We are accustomed to thinking of the Cross merely as a "religious symbol," like the Star of David or the yin-yang. Let me remind and assure you, the Cross is in no way religious. For most people living today, this concept is very hard to understand and to accept. We need to make a conscious effort to understand that the Cross in reality is, by a very long way, the most irreligious, unspiritual object ever to find its way into the heart of faith.

This fact is powerful testimony to the unique significance of the death of Christ. Always remember that crosses were placed by the roadside as a form of public announcement: these miserable beings that you see before you are not of the same species as the rest of us. The purpose of pinning the victims up like insects was to invite the gratuitous abuse of the passersby. Those crowds understood that their role was to increase, by jeering and mocking, the degradation of those who had been thus designated unfit to live.

The theological meaning of this is that crucifixion is an enactment of the worst that we are, an embodiment of the most sadistic and inhuman impulses that lie within us. The Son of God absorbed not only all of the cruelty of mankind, but He also took upon Himself all the sins of humanity.

The mocking of Jesus, the spitting and scorn, the "inversion of his kingship," the "studious dethronement" with the crown of thorns and purple robe—all were part of a deliberate procedure of shaming that unfolded in several stages, of which crucifixion itself was only the culmination. Some of the most compelling paintings of the mockery of Jesus are unsparing in their depiction of the sheer viciousness and inhumanity of the men torturing him. We see in their faces the twisted expressions of those who have lynched black people. We see the sadistic glee of those who have abused prisoners of war. We see the uncanny smiles reported to have been on the faces of the terrorist pilots who struck the World Trade Center. And if we are truly honest with ourselves this Good Friday, we see also within our own hearts the capacity, under certain circumstances, to engage in terrible acts, or to assign others to do terrible acts in our name while we wash our hands of them.[1] I believe these Seven Last Saying of Jesus Christ on the Cross transcend the First Century Church. I believe that they are meant for the Twenty First Century Church and for future generations to come.

The First Word
(Luke 23:34)

"But Jesus was saying, Father, forgive them; for they do not know what they are doing". People act surprised and often times even shocked when they hear me say that before God created the earth and before God created the Garden of Eden, He first prepared Calvary and the Cross, and agreed to surrender his only begotten son, Jesus to die for the remission of humanity's sins. Man's rebellion did not take God by surprise, nor was God caught off guard. Redemption was not an improvisation, an emergency measure in response to an unexpected setback.[2] The Apostle Peter wrote in his first letter that God has foreknowledge (I Peter 1:2). God sees things not only while they're happening, but even before they happen.

This first saying of Jesus upon the cross was Jesus' prayer for forgiveness for those who were crucifying him: the Roman soldiers, and apparently for all others who were involved in his crucifixion. In this prayer, Jesus places no limit on his forgiveness. Thus it can be reasonably assumed that in this prayer He may have been asking for forgiveness not only for the Roman soldiers or Pharisees, but also for the temple authorities and even for Judas.

Considering the likelihood that none of those who were involved in implementing Jesus' crucifixion would have fully known what they were really doing, it would seem probable that Jesus' prayer of forgiveness would have extended to each person involved."[3]

Instead of being overwhelmed and consumed with pain and misery brought on by His own suffering, Jesus asked forgiveness for all persons responsible for the evil done to Him and I believe by extension, all who ignorantly go the way of sin.

The great reversal reverses all of our preconceptions. God must become what we are in order that we might become what God is. To effectively take our part, He must take our place.

The Sermon

A Lesson on Forgiveness from the King of Kings

It's very obvious that the events of Luke 23:34 are recorded in the other New Testament Gospels, in Matthew 27:35; Mark 15:24 and John 19:23-24. However, none of the other Gospel writers Matthew, Mark or John, record this compassionate plea of Jesus from the cross. Their focus as it relates to this part of the crucifixion account centers on the crucifixion itself. The dividing of Jesus' garments and casting of lots to determine which of the four soldiers would receive Jesus' tunic. However, the Holy Spirit does not lead the other Gospel writers, Matthew, Mark or John to record anything regarding this compassionate plea.

The Gospel of Luke alone records this lesson on

forgiveness from the King of Kings. Not only was it a compassionate plea, but it is also a powerful statement. So powerful were these words, that for thirty to forty years after the crucifixion they remained on the mind and in the heart of the men and women which heard them. You see, conservative estimates state that Jesus had been crucified, died, rose from the dead and was seated on the right hand of God the Father thirty or perhaps forty years prior to Luke's arriving on the scene. Yet, while researching information regarding Christ and conducting face-to-face interviews with persons believed to have been an eyes witness to the crucifixion, Luke is consistently told by people that they remember hearing Jesus say from the cross, *"Father forgive them"*.

This is not the first time Jesus teaches a lesson on forgiveness as both God and man. The first time Jesus teaches on forgiveness is recorded in the Gospel of Matthew. You may recall in the fifth chapter of Matthew it records, *"When Jesus saw the crowds, He went up on the mountain; and after he sat down, His disciples came to him. He opened His mouth and began to teach them"* (Matthew 5:1-2). This is what is commonly referred to as "The Sermon on the Mount". It is the first time Jesus teaches publicly. It's interesting to note that the Holy Spirit leads Matthew to record that Jesus was located on a mountain as He began to teach, because the Gospel of Matthew presents Jesus as both Lord and King. A King always sits high and is lifted up above his subjects. So as king it's only natural that Jesus would deliver this first sermon from a mountain which was symbolic of His heavenly throne. In this sermon, which by the way, the other Gospel writers do not record, Jesus instructs His disciples on prayer. He says, pray, in this way, "Our Father who art in Heaven, Hallowed be your name.

Your Kingdom come. At the end of this prayer Jesus, teaches his disciples, *"For if you forgive others for their trespasses, your heavenly Father will also forgive you. But if you do not forgive others, then your Father will not forgive your trespasses"* (Matthew 6:14-15).

The second time we see Jesus teaching on forgiveness as recorded in the Word of God is at the beginning of the Week of Passion. On Friday he arrives in Bethany to spend time with Mary, Martha and Lazarus, and Mary washes his feet. On Saturday, the Sabbath, Jesus decides to rest. On Sunday, the first day of the week, Jesus rode into Jerusalem on a donkey, fulfilling the prophecy of Zechariah 9:9 *"Rejoice greatly, O daughter of Zion; shout, O daughter of Jerusalem: behold, your King cometh unto thee: he is just, and having salvation; lowly, and riding upon an ass, and upon a colt…"*

Just as the mountain had become His throne, this donkey becomes his royal coach; because every king has a royal coach or a royal carriage. And if one has a royal carriage than one has a royal procession. For the people spread their clothes in the way, and others cut down branches off the trees, and spread the branches in the way. And they that went ahead of him, and those that followed, cried saying, "Hosanna; blessed is He that come the in the name of the Lord: Blessed be the kingdom of our father David that cometh in the name of the Lord; Hosanna in the highest."

On Monday, He enters the temple, threw out those who sold and brought in the temple and declared, *"My house shall be called of all nations the house of prayer? but you have made it a den of thieves"* (Mark 11:17). Finally, on Tuesday, as it's recorded in the Gospel of Mark he once again teaches, his disciples, *"And when you stand praying, forgive if you have anything against anyone, so that your Father who is in heaven will forgive you your trespasses. But if you do not forgive; neither will your Father who is in heaven forgive your transgression"* (Mark 11:26).

Although all the Gospels record Jesus' entrance in to Jerusalem at the beginning of the Week of Passion, the Holy

Spirit directs Mark alone to record this second teaching of Jesus on forgiveness. In Matthew Jesus teaches as King while seated high on mountain. In Mark Jesus teaches as King just having entered into Jerusalem seated high on the back of a donkey.

Finally, Jesus teaches one more time on forgiveness as both God and man. Remember, none of the other Gospel writers Matthew, Mark or John, record this compassionate plea of Jesus from the cross. Their focus as it relates to this part of the crucifixion account, centers on the crucifixion itself, the dividing of Jesus' garments and casting of lots to determine which of the four soldiers would receive Jesus' tunic. But the Holy Spirit leads them to record nothing of this compassionate plea. Luke alone records this lesson on forgiveness from the King.

Though dying Jesus still teaches on forgiveness as King. Once again Jesus teaches from a position above everyone else. For, He is lifted high and stretched wide on an old wooden cross. Every king has a kingdom, and every kingdom as a crest. When we look toward America we see the bold Eagle. When we look toward Great Britain we see a Lion. When we look toward Russia we see a Bear. But, when we look toward Calvary we see The Cross.

Just as the mountain had become a symbol of Jesus' heavenly throne, the donkey a symbol of His royal coach or carriage, The Cross now becomes a symbol of His heavenly crest. Every crest bears an inscription. The inscription written over the head of Jesus in Greek, Latin and Hebrew read, "This Is the King of The Jews".

All of Christianity and I dare say the entire world, needs to thank the Devil, because an inscription becomes a lasting record. Once written it can not be changed. Finally, an inscription is meant to be established upon the memory of the reader forever and ever. "This is the King of the Jews", not this was the King of the Jews, but "This is the King of Jews". Jesus was King then and He's still King. Jesus looks down on the crowd and declares, *"Father forgive them for they know not what they do"* (Luke 23:34). Forgive Judas for his betrayal, forgive Peter of his denial, forgive Pilate of his judgment of your only begotten Son, and forgive humanity for its unbelief. Jesus teaches as King of Kings, for through obedience of His Father's will, He becomes the perfect example and application of forgiveness.

Jesus who taught forgiveness from the cross, died so that humanity might be forgiven and saved. Jesus was buried in a borrowed tomb, but on the third day morning, He rose with all power in His hand. And now Jesus sits rules and reigns as King of Kings on the right hand of God our Father, for First Epistle of John declares, "*For there are three that bear record in heaven, the Father, the King (which is the Word), and the Holy Spirit: and these three are one. And there are three that bear witness in earth, the spirit, and the water, and the blood: and these three agree in one*" (I John 5:8).

The Second Word
(Luke 23:43)

"And He said to him, "Truly I say to you, today you shall be with me in Paradise". One popular legend states that the good malefactor was to the right of Jesus, such as Matthew 25 depicts the final judgment of humanity with the goats on the left and the sheep on the right. The good malefactor perhaps represents the sheep which is found.

"Jesus is crucified between two criminals (thieves). Both of the thieves who were crucified with Christ had early on joined bystanders in mocking Jesus (Mark 15:32). The Gospel of Luke tells us, *"One of the criminals who hung there hurled insults at him: 'Aren't you the Christ? Save yourself and us!"* (Luke 23:39). This man wanted only escape from his pain.

This criminal had no desire to know Jesus as his Savior and to repent of his sins.

But, in this same Gospel, Luke reveals a miraculous change in the other criminal. He came to believe. He too had mocked Jesus earlier, but now he rebukes the other criminal. This criminal supports Jesus' innocence and asks him to remember him when he comes into his kingdom. Jesus replies to him using his set formulas for important sayings: *"Truly, I say to you..."*

Then follows the only use of the word paradise in the Gospels; as this is the word used in the Septuagint (the Greek translation of the Hebrew Bible) for the Garden of Eden.

By paradise did Christ mean that this criminal would go straight to heaven? Now, we know that wasn't the case. What Jesus did know was that in the moment after this criminal's legs were broken and he died that he would come up in presumably the second resurrection which would seem like the same day to him. At that time the earth would have been transformed into a paradise and he will have his chance to receive salvation.

Others have suggested that Jesus may have meant a return of humanity to the presence of God. However, it is traditionally meant to refer to the abode of the blessed dead. Perhaps, it can be read that the criminal's own confession of guilt opens the way to forgiveness of sin."[4] Jesus has said, *"And I, when I am lifted up from the earth, I will draw all men to myself"* (John 12:32). So through Jesus, men and women beyond numbering of every generation, nationality, ethnic group, language and culture have been drawn nearer to The Cross. It is widely believed throughout Christianity that this converted malefactor, who Catholic tradition has named *Dysmas,* by his own belief and conversion experience was drawn to The Cross and salvation by Jesus Christ. Jesus begins at the bottom of humanity.

We should not at all be surprised by this, for Jesus had so often said that the *"first shall be last and the last shall be first"* (Matthew 19:30). I believe that Jesus begins at the bottom of humanity to demonstrate that no one can fall so far they are beyond the reach of God's love.

There is a school of thought which teaches that perhaps the other thief, the one Catholic tradition has named *Gestas,* as well as, others such as Judas that did not turn toward the light, hope and belief to accept Jesus as their personal savior that death was not definitive, was not final, and was not forever. Perhaps in the end, every knee will truly bow and tongues confess including those which died refusing to do so.

Perhaps, in the end, before the great drama of salvation is complete, every man and woman and child created by God from eternity to eternity will hear Jesus say, *"Today you will be with me in paradise."* The idea that, in the end, everyone will be saved. Many theologians routinely dismiss the idea, condemning it as "universalism." But in the early centuries Christian thought it was not such a settled question. Some Greek fathers had a name for it, *apocatastasis*, by which they meant that in the end, when all is said and done, when the final curtain falls on the cosmic drama of salvation, all free moral creatures-angles, human beings and even devils—will share in the grace of salvation.

In the early centuries great Christian thinkers such as St. Gregory of Nyssa and Clement of Alexandria were sympathetic to this idea. Origen embraced the idea outright and his teaching, or what was thought to be his teaching, was condemned by the Council of Constantinople in the year 553. In the modern 21st century church the greatest teacher and supporter of this false teaching is Bishop Carlton Pearson, the former Pastor of Higher Dimensions Family Church of Tulsa.

The Sermon
From Paradise to Paradise

Careful examination of the Bible reveals that the event of Luke 23:43 are not recorded in the other New Testament Gospels. None of the other Gospel writers Matthew, Mark or John, records this compassionate promise of Jesus from the cross to the repentant criminal specifically, and humanity inclusively. Notice that I said it is a compassionate promise; therefore it is a statement of declaration. I don't recall where I was, but I recall a preacher teaching on this text, and his message was entitled, "Come Go with Me". The problem with his message was, that it violated the rules of homiletics (sermon preparation and delivery), which states that a sermon's subject must compliment its Biblical text.

"Come go with me" is a statement of command or a statement of action. The text is not a statement of command or action; it's a statement of declaration. Come is a verb, go is a verb, with is a preposition, me is a pronoun…"with me" makes up the prepositional phrase. It is clear in the text Jesus is not commanding or directing the criminals to do anything. In fact they are powerless do anything other than accept or reject Christ, and to die both physically and/or spiritually. It's true this verse speaks of three specific things in general. It speaks of Christ's presence; as well as, being in the presence of The Cross. Secondly, it speaks of an out cast sinner, who receives a promise to be with Jesus in paradise. Finally, the passages speak of hope for every believer in Jesus Christ of eternal salvation and the promise to be in His presence.

Among some scholars; as well as, laypersons, there exists a heated debate regarding Jesus' usage and meaning of the Greek word paradise [over against] the Greek word heaven. There are principally two schools of thoughts 1) Advocates of the first view contend the Greek words for paradise and heaven are two different words and therefore should not be used interchangeably; 2) advocates of the second view contend the Greek word used for paradise is simply an adjective (descriptive) word to represent heaven. I hold to the second view because of what the Apostle Paul writes in II Cor. 12:2-4 *"I know a man in Christ who fourteen years ago whether in the body I do not know, or out of the body I do not know, God knows such a man was caught up in the third heaven? And I know how such a man-whether in the body or apart from the body I do not know, was caught up into paradise"*.

Clearly, in this text the Apostle Paul uses the word heaven and paradise interchangeably, which, settles the argument as far as I'm concerned. Now there are those who argue that this is not correct because of what is recorded in the Gospel of John 20:17 regarding Jesus' appearance before Mary. *"Jesus saith unto her, Touch me not: for I am not yet ascended to my Father: but go to my brethren (the disciples), and say unto them, I ascend unto my Father, and your Father; and to my God, and your God."*

Clearly, this is three days after Jesus had spoken the words to the criminal on the cross. One should keep in mind that when Jesus arose from the dead, He did so in his resurrected body, not His previous human body. Both Jesus' spirit and the spirit of the criminal did indeed ascend on the promised day to paradise.

(Luke 23: 45) *"And when Jesus had cried with a loud voice, he said, Father, into your hands I commend my spirit."* However, there is yet a secret word, revealed within the text which reveals a promise given to man who was forced out of paradise. The promised to be restored back to paradise. The Bible teaches in Roman 5: 12 *"through one man Adam sin entered into the world, and death through sin, and so death spread to all men, because of sin."* Therefore man was taken from his original paradise the Garden of Eden. Yet through the second Adam (Jesus Christ) man has been saved and now has a right as well as a secured place in the new paradise of God.

You recall in the book of Genesis chapters one and two, it declares, *"In the beginning God created the heaven and the earth. The first day God created both Day and Night; the second day God made firmament (skyline) above the midst of the water; the third day God made seas, land and brought forth vegetation upon the earth; the fourth day God created the Sun, Moon and Stars; the fifth day God created all animal life; on the sixth day God created man: male and female He created them. God planted a garden east of Eden and God took the man which he had created and formed and placed him in the Garden of Eden. God caused trees to grow up from the ground, every tree that is pleasant to the sight, and good for food; the tree of life also was in the midst of the garden and the tree of knowledge and of good and evil. There flowed four rivers out of Eden which provided water for the*

*garden. The garden was rich with gold and everything else man would
need.*

*And the Lord God commanded the man, saying, "of every tree of the
garden you may freely eat: But of the tree of the knowledge of good and
evil, you shall not eat of it: for in the day that you eat of it you shall surely
die. And the Lord said it is not good that man should be alone; I will
make a help meet for him." So God caused a deep sleep to fall upon
Adam, and he slept: and he took one of his ribs, and closed up the flesh
instead thereof; and the rib, which the Lord God had taken from man,
made him a woman, and brought her unto the man. And Adam said
this is now bone of my bone, and flesh of my flesh: she shall be called
Woman, because she was taken out of Man.*

*Therefore shall a man leave his father and his mother, and shall
cleave unto his wife: and they shall be one flesh."* Adam and Eve had
it going on in this new paradise. They had no need of credit,
cash, or checks. They didn't have to worry about the
economy, the inflation rate; bull or bear markets. They
didn't care about the Dow Jones. The word recession never
passed their lips. Everything they needed was provided
through God.

But, that all soon changed for in chapter three of Genesis,
the serpent the beguiler of man, engaged in a conversation
with Eve, *"God hath said you shall not eat of every tree of the garden?*

And the woman said unto the serpent, we may eat of the fruit of the trees of the garden: But of the fruit of the tree which is in the midst of the garden, God hath said, you shall not eat of it, neither shall you touch it less you die". "So it came to pass that Eve ate of the tree of knowledge and of good and evil and she gave also her husband Adam to eat of the forbidden tree. So the eyes of them both were opened, and they knew that they were naked."

And so it was that God passed sentence on the serpent, on man and on the ground. And the Lord God said, *"Behold, the man is become as one of us, to know good and evil and now lest he put forth his hand, and take also of the tree of life, and eat, and live for ever: Therefore the Lord God sent him forth from the garden of Eden (God took man out of paradise) to till the ground from where he was taken."* Man lost his lease. His mortgage read canceled. He was evicted and ejected out from paradise. So God drove out the man and He placed at the east of the Garden of Eden cherubim, and a flaming sword which turned every way, to keep the way of the tree of life.

The first Adam got man evicted from paradise, but forty-two generations later we meet the second Adam (Jesus Christ), while He is yet dying on the cross, He looks upon the repentant male-factor and said, *"Today you shall be with me in paradise".*

- The first Adam cursed us, but the second Adam cured us.
- The first Adam damned us, but the second Adam delivered us.
- The first Adam got us evicted, but the second Adam made us His elect.
- The first Adam caused us to fall, but the second Adam through faith picked us up.
- The first Adam separated us spiritually from God, but the second Adam saved us.

Humanity has an inclusive promise from Jesus, in that we have a right and secure place in paradise. For John writes, these are the words *"from Jesus Christ, the faithful witness, the First born of the dead and the ruler of the Kings of the earth"* (Rev 1:5). *"I am the Alpha and the Omega, says the Lord God, who is and who was and who is to come, the Almighty"* (Rev. 1: 8). *"To the angel (Pastor) of the church in Ephesus write: he who has an ear, let him hear what the Spirit says to the churches. To him who overcome, I will grant to eat of the tree of life which is in the Paradise of God."* (Rev. 2:7).

John write of the things which I shall show you regarding the millennium reign. *"And I saw an angel come down form heaven, having the key of the bottomless pit and a great chain in his hand. And he laid hold on the dragon, that old serpent, which is the Devil, and*

Satan, and bound him a thousand years, And cast him into the bottomless pit, and shut him up, and set a seal upon him, that he should deceive the nations no more, till the thousand years should be fulfilled: and after that he must be loosed a little season" (Rev. 20:1-3). *"And I saw a new heaven and a new earth: for the first heaven and the first earth were passed away; and there was no more sea. And I John saw the holy city Jerusalem, coming down from God out to the heaven, prepared as a bride adorned for her husband"* (Rev 21:1-2).

"And he showed me a pure river, of water of life, clear as a crystal, proceeding out of the throne of God and of the Lamb. In the midst of the street of it, and on either side of the river, was there the tree of life (which was in the midst of the Paradise of God), which bare twelve manner of fruits, and yielded her fruit every month: and the leaves of the tree were for the healing of the nation." (Rev.22:1-2). "Blessed are they that do his commandments that they may have right to the tree of life (in the midst of the paradise of God), and may enter in through the gates into the city."

The Third Word
(St. John 19:26-27)

"When Jesus then saw His mother, and the disciple whom He loved standing nearby, He said to His mother, "Woman, behold, your son!" Then He said to the disciple, "Behold, your mother!" From that hour the disciple took her into his own household."

Jesus entrusts Mary, his mother, into the care of a disciple. Traditionally, this is thought to be John the Evangelist, but he is only referred to as the beloved disciple. The Catholic Church interprets this phrase beyond just the disciple, saying that Jesus was giving his mother to all the church, and consequently all of the church to her. The Catholic Church also uses this saying as a proof that Mary did not have any other children, because if she did have other sons who could have taken care of her, Jesus would not have needed to give her over to his beloved disciple—indeed, had Mary had other sons, such a transfer would have been incredibly insulting to them in the context of 1st century Jewish culture.

Scripture clearly reveals that Mary did indeed have other sons—James, Joses, Simon and Judas (not *Iscariot*). Protestants and evangelical reject both of the Catholic interpretations, making mention of the fact that Jesus found it necessary to take this step only because Mary's other children were not yet believers in him as Messiah. The Apostle Paul notes in 1 Corinthians 15:7 that Jesus appeared to His brother James after His resurrection and this is probably when he and his brothers began to believe that Jesus was the Messiah and resurrected Christ; as they were with Mary and the Apostles in Acts 1:14 when a replacement was chosen for Judas *Iscariot*. James became the leader of the Jerusalem church while it's believed Judas the brother of Jesus or Jude later wrote the epistle of Jude.

Yet a weaker view suggest that Jesus, on the verge of giving up his life and having given up everything else in his life, was now giving up his last "possession," which was his mother. Thus, he would be dying in absolute poverty, without even the benefit of a mother."[5]

The Sermon
Between the Womb and the Tomb

Scripture clearly reveals that the event of John 19:26-
27 are not recorded in the other New Testament Gospels.
None of the other Gospel writers Matthew, Mark or
Luke, records this tender moment shared between John,
Mary and Jesus. It has been said that "Time is that space
between the womb and the tomb. Didn't seek it. Didn't
choose, but it's up to us to use. We must suffer it we lose
it. Give account if we abuse it. Just a tiny little minute,
only sixty seconds in it. Divinity ordained it, but eternity
has claimed it" (Unknown author). Life is but a fleeting
moment. Here today, gone tomorrow. The Psalmist
declares "*Lord, make me to know my end, And what is the extent*

of my days; Let me know how transient (short-lived, brief, passing) I am" (Psalm 39:4).

The book of Job records, *"Man's days are determined, you have decreed (God has set) the number of his (man's) months and has set limits he can not exceed"* (Job 14:5). Man can argue, complain and try to cheat death all he wants, but when our time is up, it's up. It's wise to live each and everyday as if it were your last.

You and I know our birth date, only because someone has told us the actual date of our birth. We know the exact year, month, day, hour and minute of our birth. But, we do not know our death date. We do not know the exact year, month, day, hour or minute of our death. Not even in cases regarding extreme illnesses can doctors predict with certainty the exact time of a person's death.

Have you ever considered how most of us would act if God told us the exact date and time which we would die? How different would we act and live, if we knew the exact time of our death? Some of us, it not all of us would wake up in the morning thinking that if we stayed in bed death might pass us by, or if we stayed awake all night death would pass us over.

In examining the life of Jesus, we see a person who knew

not only his birth date, but also his death date. Jesus knew the exact year, month, day, hour, minute and second he would be born and die. Jesus knew how much time, that is to say, he knew the exact number of His human days. Therefore, He knew exactly how much time He had between the womb and the tomb. Not only this, but Jesus knew everything He had to accomplish between the womb and the tomb. Jesus' calendar was prepared in Heaven, but executed on earth.

Jesus kept each and every appointment. His calendar of events between the *womb* and the *tomb* were never changed. His scheduled was followed as designed by His Father. Items were never added or deleted. He never arrived too early or too late. Jesus was always on time. Items were not pushed back nor pushed forward. Between the *womb* and the *tomb* Jesus never juggled a single thing.

Although, Jesus' conception was very difference than ours, that is to say, he was conceived by and through the Holy Spirit His birth process was identical to ours. Mary his mother carried him a full nine months, and she delivered him through natural child birth. The custom of that time period was breast feeding, so Jesus was breast fed by Mary.

In the Judaic tradition until a male reached the age of

twelve years old his mother had full charge of developing, training and educating the child. After this period the father took charge of the male for the male was now considered a man. Jesus' situation may have been somewhat different. We know Joseph, Jesus' earthly dad more than likely died at an early age. Many theologians believe it was sometime after Jesus' turned twelve years of age. Luke 2:41-52 record the last occasion which Joseph is actually mentioned. Jesus alone with his parents had traveled from Nazareth to Jerusalem in observance of the Feast of Passover, and while returning back to Nazareth Joseph and Mary discover Jesus' absence.

It was the custom for males under the age of thirteen years of age to travel in the rear of the caravan, alone with the women and other children, while the men traveled in front. This is perhaps the primary reason why Jesus' disappearance went unnoticed by both Joseph and Mary. After checking with relatives and friends, Joseph and Mary decide to go back to Jerusalem to search for their son. After three days they found Him in the Temple, listening and asking teachers questions, and at the same time He answered their questions.

When asked by Mary as to why he had wandered off. His answer was immediate and unrehearsed. "Why did you seek me? Didn't you know, (as I knew, that at this appointed time between the *womb* and the *tomb)*, that I would be here doing my Father's business in my Father's house?"

Jesus knew when he would be baptized by John the Baptist. He knew that He would be led of Holy Spirit into the wilderness to be tempted by the Devil. Jesus was already prepared to have his physical desires, desire for worldly power and fame, desire for false worship all tested, between the *womb* and the *tomb*. Once again, His reply is immediate and unrehearsed. *"It is written man shall not live by bread alone, but by every word of God. It is written thou shall worship the Lord your God and Him only shall you serve. It is said thou shall not tempt the Lord your God"* (Matthew 4:4).

After being tempted of the Devil, Jesus returned to Nazareth entered the synagogue, read from the Prophecy of Isaiah and declared, *"The Spirit of the Lord is upon me, because he hath anointed me to preach the Gospel to the poor. He hath sent me to heal the broken-hearted, and give recovering of sight to the blind, to set at liberty them that are bruised, to preach the acceptable year of the Lord"* (Luke 4:18-19). For three and half-years between the *womb* and the *tomb*, Jesus accomplished all that His Father had sent Him to perform.

1). He called his twelve disciples.

2). He established the church.

3). He healed the sick, raised the dead, gave comfort to the disturbed and disturbed the comfortable.

4). He restored sight to blind. He freed the oppressed.

5). He preached every sermon he was called to preach. He prayed every prayer.

We now see Jesus in our text St John 19:26-27, as His physical attention now turns toward his mother Mary and John the disciple which he loves. The saints of yester-year use to say, and some still do, that a child sure sees hard times if momma is no longer around or when momma dies, for nobody loves a child like momma loves a child.

Jesus, while yet dying on the cross allows His mind to flashback to all that Mary, His mother, had meant and done for Him between the womb and the tomb. Jesus remembers that He was birthed from Mary's womb. It was Mary who nursed Him and changed his diapers. It was Mary who bathed Him, clothed and fed Him. It was Mary who educated, instructed and read the Word of God to Him. It was Mary who cared for, looked out for and mentored him.

Mary witnessed Jesus' first miracle, the turning of water

into wine. It was Mary who supported her son between the *womb* and the *tomb*. Mary heard the angry crowd shout out "free Barabbas, but crucify Jesus". Mary was in the crowd as Jesus was led to Calvary's cross. Mary heard the nails being driven in Jesus' hands and feet. Mary heard her son scream out each and every time a nail was driven into his body. Now, Mary watches and cries at the foot of the cross on behalf of her dying son. Dying on the cross Jesus draws near to completing all He was sent to do by his Father. With his last few words Jesus remembers Mary his momma, who had been by His side. Realizing that Joseph His earthly father has long been deceased, Jesus gives the care of Mary, his mother to the one whom He loves and trust. He gives John his youngest disciple the responsibility of caring for Mary.

Aren't you glad that before the womb and the tomb, yet while still in Heaven, Jesus decided to come to earth and dwell among mankind in the form of God and man. Jesus decided to die a sinner's death by bearing all the sins of humanity. Jesus decided to die on a Friday, preach deliverance to the captive. He disturbed the grave, defeated, and conquered death and on the third day morning after the womb and tomb, Jesus got up! He arose from the tomb and death with all power, all power in his hand.

The Fourth Word
(Matt: 27:46)

"And about the ninth hour Jesus cried out with a loud voice, saying "Eli, Eli, la ma sabach thani?" that is "My God, My God, why have you forsaken me?" The Apostle Paul perhaps referred to this moment when he wrote in 2 Corinthians 5:21: *"For He made Him who knew no sin to be sin for us, that we might become the righteousness of God in Him."* At this moment the Father placed on Him the sins of humanity to be paid as He was about to die.

During his entire adult life, Jesus had an intimate and vibrant relationship with God as His Father. Suddenly, while suffering the agony and fatigue of crucifixion, Jesus could no longer feel that wonderful heavenly Presence. At this

PREACHING THE SEVEN LAST SAYINGS
OF JESUS CHRIST ON THE CROSS

moment He could empathize with all of us when we feel separated from God because of our sins and guilt.

Of the seven sayings of Jesus from the cross, this one stands out. It is the only saying recorded in Matthew and Mark, and is the only one that appears in two parallel accounts. Intriguingly, this saying is given in Aramaic with a translation (originally in Greek) after it. This phrase also appears on the opening line of Psalm 21 in the Holy Scripture and (Psalm 22 in the Masoretic text).

In the verses immediately following this saying, in both Gospels, some who hear Jesus' cry imagine that He is calling for help from Elijah. The slight differences between the two Gospel accounts are most probably due to dialect. Matthew's version seems to have been influenced more by Hebrew, whereas Mark's is perhaps more colloquial.[6]

Many Christian believe that the quotation presents Psalm 22 as a prophecy of Christ's suffering (verses 14-18), of his message and, as a whole of his exaltation (verse 24). Some theologians claim the Father seems to have deserted the Son (v. 1-2, and the contrast between v. 5 and 6) but saves Jesus ultimately and with Him those who seek him. Thus some Christians argue that by uttering this single question Jesus was in a way announcing the whole Gospel as the moment of its decisive event (cf. Luke 4:21). This gulf of separation that occurs between God the Father and God the Son, in the death of the latter, has been described by the theologian Jurgen Moltmann as "death in God".

The Sermon
When the Righteous Seem Forsaken

Now, if you would be so kind as to examine verses 46 from the amplified Bible. *"And about the ninth hour (three o'clock) Jesus cries with a loud voice, Eli, Eli la ma sabach thani? That is My God, My God, why have you abandoned me (leaving me helpless, forsaking and failing me in my need)?"* Saints there is cause for both alarm and concern. For we are living in a time and age in which humanity is being threaten by major calamities. All across this nation we continue to hear reports of major flooding, earthquakes, famine, sickness and death.

Trouble my brothers and sisters, seems to be on every side. The myth held by many separatist, those who would separate the human race by ethnic, racial, religious, social, educational and financial status, that there is no common link between races, genders, ethnic groups and religious groups is invalidated by trouble. For surely trouble is one common denominator linking all of humanity. If trouble hasn't hit your home, don't think it's because you're immune to it. I can assure you, trouble knows your address. Things may be going well now, but we all need to be prayerful and mindful, the sea is always calm, just before the storm. The sun may be shining in your life, but a storm is raging in someone else's life.

If you don't believe me just ask brother Job. My former Pastor Dr. H. Beecher Hicks, author of the highly acclaimed book entitled, "Preaching Through a Storm", put it this way "We are either headed into a storm, in the eye of a storm, coming out of a storm, only to head back into another storm." Trouble is real.

I am not trying to disturb your peace or interrupt your comfort. I realize that most of you, if not all of you came out expecting to hear a word, a resurrection word. You didn't come out to hear a word of gloom or doom. Therefore, having knowledge of this, I feel it's necessary to state at the beginning of this discourse, I understand many came to hear a word of hope and a word of encouragement, a word of revival, a word of salvation.

Many came searching for a balm in Gilead, to heal your wounded mind, heart and soul. All week long someone has been hurting, you've been told by your doctor that something isn't right on the inside and immediate medical treatment is necessary. Others may have come to have your souls refreshed one more time by drinking from the spring of living waters, and eating from the bread of life. Many like Elijah came to sit under the juniper tree, seeking rest from life's disappointments, fears, and sorrows. You are not at all interested in any sermon which would remind you of life's problems, heartaches, headaches, challenges and struggles.

Yet, in reading the text, in reading verse 46, I am led to believe that no serious Bible student, preacher or theologian skilled in the area of hermeneutics and equipped with the principles and processes of biblical interpretation could exegete this text or analyze these verses and not be alarmed. What serious minded Bible reader could read these passages and not be alarmed. The problem however, with many people is that they read the Bible like it's a novel or some other paper back book. The Bible is not a book in which you should just allow your eyes, but never your mind to act upon what is being read. I fail to see how any one could read these verses, and derive or conclude a message of hope or see a picture of encouragement.

The verses follow and are themselves the story of the passion and passing of the King of Kings. To say that is to recognize the emotional difficulty of exposition and interpretation of the text. For you see there are issues regarding the crucifixion which are too profound for words, things that can not be fully apprehended or comprehended by our finite minds. We lack the intelligence to fully understand all the events of Calvary. Here, as never before in the reading of Matthew's Gospel we see the King of Kings, Jesus Christ, The Anointed in a state of loneliness which defies explanation. Some may be asking "What Jesus is he talking about?" Surely, he's not talking about the Alpha and Omega, the Lily of the Valley, the Prince of Peace, the Bright and Morning Star, the Bridge over Trouble Waters, our All and All. Oh! Yes I am. I'm talking about your Jesus and my Jesus. The Alpha and Omega, the Lily of the Valley, the Prince of Peace, the Bright and Morning Star, the Bridge over Trouble Waters, our All and All I'm talking about Jesus, who appeared to be left alone.

Does any one recall a time in which you were or you felt

like you were all alone and helpless. Have you ever felt abandoned, isolated cast off and cast out? Has anyone ever abandoned you? Has anyone ever left you when you needed them? Has anyone ever left you? Has anyone ever left you holding the bag? Has anyone promised you, "They would be with you through thick and through thin, but just as things got thick they got..." You know the rest. "They got thin". For the first time in His human existence, Jesus feels and is all alone. Where was Peter, Andrew, James, Philip, Bartholomew, Matthew, Thomas, James, Simon and Judas the Brother of James? Where were they? Now, I know what you biblical scholars are thinking!

You're probably saying to yourself, "well brother Preacher, according to John's Gospel, John, Mary, Elisabeth, Mary Magdalene and Mary the wife of Cleophas were there"! They were present at Calvary. You're absolutely correct, they were at Calvary. But, let's examine the complete biblical record. The Bible says in John 19:25, "*...they stood at the cross of Jesus.*" All they did was stand at the cross. They did nothing else, but stand at the cross of Jesus. Has anybody in here ever gotten into a fight and needed your friends standing by to jump in and give you a hand, but all they did was simply stand by and watch you get the worst beating of your life? You needed them to help you, but all they did was stand by and watch. Well, John, Mary and those with them simply stood at the cross and watched.

Yes! They showed up at Calvary, that's all they did, they showed up to simply to watch. None of them even had the good sense to cry out on Jesus' behalf. They stood before God Himself and lacked the courage to even pray. That's all they did was show up.

That's what wrong with many churches today! They're filled with too many folks who just show up. We don't need any more folks joining church just to show up. But what we need are folk who will show up and then show out. Every now and then when folk show up to church they ought to smile, have a pat in their foot, give a testimony, have a song in their heart, a prayer on their lips. They ought to do something for Jesus. They ought to do something to "turn the world upside down". When trouble hits I don't need folk to just show up. I need some folk to show up and then show out.

I need some folk who know how to get a prayer through. I need some strong prayer warriors, some folk who have been on the battlefield a long time. I need some folk who know how to get in contact with God. I need some folk to remind me God promised, *"I'm the head and not the tail"* (Deuteronomy 28:13). I'm above and not below. I need some folk to tell me *"one can chase a thousand, but two can put ten thousand to flight"* (Deuteronomy 32:30). I need some folk who will show up and then show out. John, Mary and the others with them showed up, to show up. When people show up to show up, the person is still left all alone. Jesus was still all alone emotionally and spiritually.

So, I ask again where were all the folks, which Jesus healed and brought back from the dead? Where was the man who had been demon-possessed but set free by Jesus? Where was Simon's mother-in-law who Jesus cured of fever? Where was the man Jesus healed of palsy? Where was the woman who touched His robe and was healed from bleeding? Where was Lazarus, whom Jesus raised from the dead?

Where was the centurion whose daughter was raised from the dead? Where were they, when a crown of thorns was placed upon his head? Where were they, when He was being despised, rejected of men and spit upon? Where were they, when He was being wounded for their transgressions and our transgressions? Where were they, when He was being bruised for their iniquities and our iniquities? Where were they, when He was being nailed to the cross? Where were they, when He was being beaten? Where were they, when He was pierced in His side? Where were they when they crucified our Lord, and King of Kings? They all abandoned Him and left Him all alone. Jesus was cut off from people and cut off, more importantly, from His Heavenly Father. That's part of what He meant by, "*I and the Father are one*" (John 10:30). However, in order to carry out the divine plan of salvation, God had to cut off, at least temporarily His divine relationship with His only begotten Son.

Allow me to share with you quickly the definition for Expository Preaching once again. It is the communication of a biblical concept derived from and transmitted through a historical, grammatical, and literary study of a passage, in its context, which the Holy Spirit first applies to the personality and experience of the preacher, then through the preacher to the hearer. If this is what Expository Preaching is made of, then any attempt to describe and explain these passages alarms me.

All I'm trying to say church is that preachers should, when preparing their sermons first identify with all the characters in the text. Secondly, we should bring to bear some past or present event in our own life to serve as an example for the congregation. The challenge presented by these verses, brings us to the point of asking, "What historical event known to man, past, present or future can compare to the events of Calvary?" Keeping in mind what was previously stated, there are matters and events which happened at Calvary which are too profound for words— things that can not be fully comprehended or apprehended by our finite minds. So, it would seem to the world that the righteous are then forsaken.

What grammatical or literary work, what poem, what song, what play, what movie, work known to man conveys and gives a complete understanding and comprehensive insight to all the events of Calvary? What theologian, what scientist, or historian can you call to share with you all the mysteries of Calvary? I know of none, because there are none.

What experience have you had which equal, compares to or even relates to the events of Calvary? I don't know about you but I have none. Since none of us know of no work, no writing, no song, no movie, no person or anything else which can fully explain all the events of Calvary, it seems clear then to the world that the righteous are forsaken. As the world reads these verses, the language of the text implies to them that God Himself forsook Jesus. The language of the text implies that God did indeed abandon Jesus, and left Him alone. It appears that the Gospel writer has given Satan, the Prince of the power of the Air, prince of the underworld, ruler of the nations of this world, the accuser of the brethren, the very power he needs to destroy Christianity. For there are many who stand in opposition to God's divine and inspired Word, who seek to prove that God did indeed forsake his son, and as a result Jesus never rose from the grave.

From such heresies and false teaching has emerged the "new age" movement whose members believe that all truth is hidden in the consciousness of man. They believe that man has the power to control his consciousness; therefore, man himself is a god.

From such false teachings, cults such as the Jehovah Witnesses, who deny the Father-Son relationship and who also deny that Jesus was fully God have come into existence. Anyone who denies the God-head of Jesus Christ the Bible says, that "*person is the Anti-Christ*" (I John 2:22).

From such false teachings have emerged uninspired and unholy writings such as the Q'ran held by Muslim to be

God's final revealed word, and the book of Mormons, viewed by followers of Joseph Smith as God's final and only revealed word. And so, my brothers and sisters through the eyes of the world and non-Christians, through the false teaching and writings from the enemies of God's true revealed and divine Holy Scriptures it would seem that Jesus was forsaken and that the righteous then are forsaken.

In order to understand the text, to begin to understand what Jesus is conveying in the text, we must be brave enough to go beyond the literal translation of the text. The literal translation of the text seems to suggest that Jesus was indeed abandoned by God. But, to go beyond the text is to get in harmony with the text or simply put, we must harmonize the text.

The manner in which Scripture is harmonized is by comparing it to or relating it to other Scripture contain in the Bible. The point which Jesus makes is that when going through dark times, *God must still be our God*. Look at verse 46. Jesus cried with a loud voice, My God, My God. Church, if I am not mistaken the word "my" in the King's English is used in the possessive case, to show ownership. The word "my" is personal. It means the thing to which it refers *belongs to me*. Jesus, even while dying knew that God was still His

Father, and that He was still the only begotten Son. There are ministries all over this nation teaching their members to just *name it and claim it*. We all have heard these TV preachers shouting at the top of their lungs, *"name it and claim it all in the name of Jesus"*.

I don't have a particular problem with claiming promises given us by God, but everything in the Bible is not meant for us to claim. *But that's a different sermon.* The point that I wish to make however, to some Christians and some of those TV preachers who shout, *"Name it and claim it"* is this, don't forget to claim God when you're down. Don't forget to claim God, when you're broke. Don't forget to claim God when you lose your job. Don't forget to claim God when folks have forsaken you. Don't forget to claim God when folks have cast you off, put you down, left you out, left you behind, pushed you back, put you off.

Even through the darkest of times, *God must still be your God*. God must be your Jehovahjireh (He who provides), God must be your Jehovahrapha (He who heals), and God must be your Jehovahnissi (He who is your banner). God must be your Jehovah-shalom (He who is your peace). Saints, God must be your all in all.

When the righteous seem forsaken, cry out unto God.

When you feel all alone, just cry out unto God. When you feel abandoned; cry out unto God. When the world has cast you off, cry out unto God When friends forsake you, cry out unto God. When you've been cast down cry out unto God. When you've been left behind cry out unto God. When you've been pushed back cry out unto God. When you've been forgotten, cry out unto God; and God will hear your cry.

- Abraham cried unto God and God heard his cry.
- Jacob cried unto God and God heard his cry.
- Isaac cried unto God and God heard his cry.
- Joseph cried unto God and God heard his cry.
- Moses cried unto God, and God heard his cry.
- Joshua cried unto God and God heard his cry.
- David cried unto God and God heard his cry.
- Elijah cried unto God and God hear his cry.
- Job cried unto God and God hear his cry.
- Daniel cried unto God and God heard his cry.
- Jeremiah cried unto God and God heard his cry.
- Ezekiel cried unto God and God heard his cry.
- Jesus cried unto God and God heard his cry.

You need to know today that God hears your cry. You need to believe that God hears your cry. You need to feel like God hears your cry. I am glad today that God heard my cry. I am glad today that God heard Jesus' cry. God heard His cry from Calvary's cross; where they hung Him high, and stretched Him wide. God heard His cry as blood flowed from His side. God heard His cry when He said Father, *"Forgive them for they know not what they do."* God heard His cry when He said Father, *"It is finished, into thy hands I commend my spirit."*

There may be those here today, who have never heard about this man named Jesus, or you may have heard just a little. You need to hear a "resurrection Word". There was a man named Jesus who came through forty and two generation. You may have heard he was born in a stable to Mary and Joseph. You may have heard that, *"He came unto His own, but His own received Him not; but to those who received Him, He gave the power to become the sons of God* (John 1:12).

You may have heard that He healed the sick and raised the dead. You may have heard that He healed the cripple and restored sight unto the bind. You may have heard that He turned water into wine and that He walked on the water. You may have heard that He spoke to a raging sea and said, *"Peace be still*. You may have heard that He fed 5000 with just two fish and a five loaves of bread. You may have heard that He was tried for treason and found guilty by man, though no guilt was in Him.

You may have heard that a crown of thorns was placed upon His head. You may have heard that He was beaten, spit on and rejected by men. You may have heard that He was led to a place called Golgotha's hill. You may have heard that He was nailed to a wooden cross by His hands and feet. You may have heard that He was pierced in His side. You may have heard that He died; I said He died and was buried in Joseph tomb.

You may have heard that sin called up death and said, "Now you're in charge". You may have may have heard that death called up the grave and said, "Now you have the victory". You may have heard that Hell got happy and Satan began to relax.

But, what you may not have heard, I said what you may not have heard is that early, early, Easter morning God spoke to death and said, "death where is thy sting"? Grave, "where is thy victory"? Satan "your days are numbered". Then God called to His Son, saying "Arise", "Arise". Jesus, got up with all power, all power in Heaven and in Earth.

- Power to resurrect dead marriages.
- Power to resurrect spiritually dead relationships.
- Power to resurrect spiritually dead churches.
- Power to resurrect joy.
- Power to resurrect sick bodies.
- Power to resurrect confused minds.
- Power to heal broken hearts.
- Power to restore peace.
- Power to comfort the disturbed.
- Power to disturb the comfortable.
- Power to make wrong right.
- Power to fix what's broken.
- Power to fight your battles.

I've seen the lighting flashing. I've heard the thunder roar. Like a tree planted beside the still water, I will not be moved. I'm not going to faint, nor grow weary. I won't slow down, lie down, or sit down. I'm going to run until I see what the end will be. I'm going run on until I see what the end will be. Are you're going to run on, are you're going to run on? Until, until you see what the end will be? Aren't you glad Jesus arose from the dead…so, like King David, I can say that I have never, never, never, not ever, seen the righteous forsaken nor their seed begging bread. I am glad that Jesus was temporarily forsaken. He had to be temporarily forsaken, so that we could be permanently forgiven. Jesus had to be cast down, so that we could be caught up. He had to be put down, so that we could be lifted up. He had to be put off, so that we could put on. He had to be lied on so that we could know the truth. He had to be rejected so that we would be accepted. Jesus had to die…so that we could live with Him forever.

The Fifth Word
(St. John 19:28)

"*After this, Jesus knowing that all things were now accomplished, that the scripture might be fulfilled, saith, I thirst.*" The time of final sacrifice is near. Jesus had endured and overcome the heat, pain, rejection and loneliness. He could have suffered and died in silence. Instead, unexpectedly, he asked for help. "Knowing that all was now completed, and so that the Scripture would be fulfilled, Jesus said, "I thirst".

Earlier Jesus had been offered the same drink but with added gall. Jesus refused it as recorded in Matthew 27:34. Why refuse it earlier and now take a drink at the moment of death? The narcotic drink would have helped deaden the pain, but Jesus refused it. He drank the cup of suffering instead. Instead of reaching for a comforter Jesus, was prepared to take the difficult but necessary path. When finally He had fully drank of the cup of suffering; He then asked for a drink...or does He? After all why would Jesus, who is one with the Chief Comforter (The Holy Spirit) need a narcotic drink to be comforted?

The Sermon
A Thirst for Glory

It goes without saying, the event of John 19:28 are not recorded in the other New Testament Gospels. None of the other Gospel writers Matthew, Mark or Luke, records this agonizing cry of Jesus from the cross, "*I thirst*".

It is agonizing because it is not a cry of physical thirsting, but rather a cry of spiritual thirsting. One might ask how I can make such a statement. A statement which suggests, that Jesus was not physically thirsty. I can make the statement because all one has to do is harmonize the verse with the Word of God. In other words, compare Scripture against itself.

Although the other Gospel writers make no mention of

this agonizing cry, "I thirst", they do, however, record that Jesus was offered and given vinegar mixed with gall to drink. Not only Jesus, but anyone who was crucified was given this mixture, not to satisfy one's thirst, but rather to help ease the physical pain of the wounds inflicted on the human body. Mark 15:36 *"And one ran and filled a sponge full of vinegar, and put it on a reed, and gave him to drink."* Luke 23:36 *"And the soldiers also mocked him, coming to him, and offering him vinegar"*. John 19:29 *"Now there was set a vessel full of vinegar: and they filled a sponge with vinegar, and put it upon hyssop, and put it to his mouth."*

These passages clearly state that Jesus was given the mixture of vinegar and gall to drink; however; Matthew 27:34 says *"They gave him vinegar to drink mixed with gall: and when he had tasted it, he would not drink."* When Jesus had tasted it, he would not drink.

Now, I don't care how bad something tastes when I'm thirsty, like most people I will drink to satisfy my thirst. I realize that some may not be totally convinced that this was not a physical thirsting. Well you may recall the Bible declares, *"Jesus was led up by the Spirit into the wilderness to be tempted of the Devil. And when he had fasted forty days and forty nights, he was afterward hungered"* (Matt.4:1-2).

This clearly reveals that Jesus became physically hungry;

however, the Gospels make no mention or give any reference of his being thirsty. Scripture is silence on this point. There are scholars who assert or suggest that he must have drank something, because He was fully man and no human can survive without liquid beyond three or perhaps four days in the dessert. However, these same scholars fail to acknowledge the fact that while Jesus was fully man, he was also fully God, and as such was capable of surviving without food or water for forty days and forty nights.

Besides Mark 1:12 records "...*and the angels ministered unto him*". How they ministered unto him, how they helped him, we do not know. The Scriptures neither implicitly nor explicitly state that Jesus drank liquids during this period. I believe that if Jesus could go without liquids for forty days and forty nights, I believe he was more than capable of enduring six hours on the cross, for Mark 15:25 records "*And it was the third hour, and they crucified him*".

Mark 15:34 "And at the ninth hour Jesus cried out with a loud voice, saying..." So, once again I believe this is a cry of spiritual thirsting. Now the question becomes what was it that Jesus spiritually thirsted? I believe he thirst for his glory! In Exodus 33:18-21 we find these words, "*Then Moses said, "I pray You, show me Your GLORY!" And He (Lord) said, "I Myself*

will make all My goodness pass before you, and will proclaim the name
of the Lord before you; and I will be gracious to whom I will be gracious,
and will show compassion on whom I will show compassion." But He
said, "You cannot see My face, for no man can see me and live." Get
this: Moses asked God to show him his glory, and God
replies, "You can not see My face, no man can see Me and
live". This is why it's so difficult to convince some people
that Jesus was fully God and fully man. They attempt to lift
this verse up as evidence to support their claim and their
view that Jesus was simply fully man, but not God.

Their argument asserts that literally thousands of people
beheld Jesus face to face, yet they did not die. Therefore,
Jesus could not have been partially or fully God. So, how is
it Christians can assert and uphold with great belief that
Jesus was indeed fully God and fully man? How it is that
humanity could see and behold Jesus and not die? Because
Jesus emptied Himself of Himself.

If I asked every person in here to raise your hand if you
have gas in your car, everyone in here who drove tonight
would be able to raise your hand. Notice I didn't ask if you
had a full tank, half of a tank, or a quarter of a tank. I simply
asked if you had gas in your car. Furthermore, if you were
able to drive your car and not run out of gas prior to arriving

to church and your gas needle reflects that you're not on empty, then you still have gas in your tank. You burned off some of the gas while driving to church; however, you didn't burn off all of the gas.

Just as you burned off some of the gas while driving to church Jesus had to first empty Himself of part of His full glory. He did not empty Himself of His deity. He simply emptied Himself of His full glory. He came to earth with only part of His glory. Tell your neighbor; Jesus still had some glory in His tank. That's what God allowed Moses to see. Moses saw only the back side of God's glory.

John 17:1-5 *"Jesus spoke these things; and lifting up His eyes to heaven, He said, "Father, the hour has come; glorify your Son, that the Son may glorify you, even as You gave Him authority over all flesh, that to all whom You have given Him, he may give eternal life. "This is eternal life, that they may know you, the only true God, and Jesus Christ whom you have sent. "I glorified you on the earth, having accomplished the work which you have given me to do. "Now, Father, glorify me together with yourself, with the glory which I had with you before the world was". Glorify me together, with yourself, with the glory which I had.*

The word "had" means you once, owned you once possessed, you once held something, but now, you no longer have it. Jesus no longer had His full glory. He now longs for the time when He would once again possess His full glory.

We see our Lord on the cross. He is fully God and fully man. Yet, he must die as fully man only, because God can not die. The only way for Him to die as fully man is for Him to give up, surrender, to empty Himself of all of the glory He has left.

So, Jesus surrenders now His full glory and says, "I thirst". Aren't you glad tonight, that He thirsted? Aren't you glad that He died? But, in that He died, early on the third day morning, He arose from the dead. For John wrote in Revelation 5:12 *"Worthy is the Lamb that was slain to receive, power, and riches, and wisdom, and strength, and honor, and glory, and blessing."* He who emptied Himself of His full glory received His full glory and much more, from God His Father.

The Sixth Word
(St. John 19:30)

"When Jesus therefore had received the vinegar, he said. It is finished: and he bowed his head, and gave up the ghost." The sixth saying of Christ on the cross is one of triumph. Jesus did not whisper, *"It is finished,"* as one who has been defeated, broken and battered and forced to admit defeat. He shouted it like a conqueror who has won his final engagement with the enemy and as one who brings a tremendous task to triumphant conclusion. Even so, Jesus' humility rings in His words. His was not a vain, I showed you attitude. He did not even say, "I did it" or "I did it my way". Jesus claimed no credit. To the end, Jesus' mind was on the work He came to do. Jesus came to do a work. He came to create a new race

of people, a new creation. Jesus said, "*I must work the work of him that sent me, while it is day*" (John 9:4). Jesus did not come to earth to rest. He came to complete the work of redemption.

He triumphantly announced, for all to hear, "*It is finished*".

But it is not over. From now until it reaches its final consummation in the coming of God's kingdom the human story, including all its suffering and tears, is gathered up and redeemed in the cross of Christ.

The Sermon
The Legacy of the Church

None of the other Gospel writers Matthew, Mark or Luke, records this profound statement of Jesus from the cross, *"It is finished."* In this passage of Scripture, Jesus signs, seals and delivers His legacy to the Church. The world should not be surprised that Jesus remembered The Church, His future bride (Revelations 21:9). After all Jesus leaves with His Heavenly Father the request that God forgives those responsible for His crucifixion (Luke 23:34). To the soldiers which led him to the Chief Priests and Pilate to be examined by them, He left His garment which was torn into four pieces, and His coat also which was left to the winner of the tossed lots (St. John 19:23-24).

To the repentant malefactor Jesus leaves the promise of being with Him in paradise (Luke 23:43. Jesus leaves the care of Mary his mother with His beloved disciple, John (John 19:27). To Mary his mother, Jesus leaves a new son, John His disciple (John 19:26). And finally Jesus commends His own spirit into the hand of God His Father (Luke 23:46).

If this were our eulogy, people might say that we handled a few things worthy of mention before the end arrived; however, could they say or even fully agree that we legitimized our last will and testament? But of Jesus it can be said, even if not fully agreed, He did indeed legitimize His last will and testament. In this statement of inheritance, this bequeath, He affirms to God His Father and to humanity that all which He was sent to perform has been completed. In three and half-years of ministry Jesus accomplished all that His Father had sent Him to perform (just to name a few).

1). He was baptized by John the Baptist

2). He called his twelve disciples.

3). He established the church.

4). He healed the sick, raised the dead, gave comfort to the disturbed and disturbed the comfortable.

5). He restored sight to the blind. He freed the oppressed. He fed the hungry.

6). He performed every miracle.

7). He rebuked the Pharisees, Sadducees, Scribes and other religious rulers.

8). He kept every appointment, entered every city and region ordained even before time.

9). He preached every sermon he was called to preach. He prayed every prayer the Spirit of God placed on His heart.

As believers we know, *It is finished*, because the writer of Hebrew declares, *"God who at sundry times, and in divers manners, spoke in times past unto the fathers by the prophets, hath in these last days, spoken unto us by His Son, Jesus Christ."* God provided grace, but Jesus personified grace.

One day, Grace stepped out, and then grace stepped down,

Grace stepped through, forty-two generations,

Grace put on a mortal body,

Grace was born in Bethlehem,

Grace was wrapped in swaddling clothes,

Grace was laid in a manger,

Grace was baptized in the river Jordan,

Grace was despised by the world,

Grace was doubted by His disciples,

Grace was forsaken by His family and friends,

Grace was oppressed by His enemies,

Then One Thursday, Grace came under fire and attack,

On Thursday, Grace was arrested like a criminal,

On Thursday, Grace was beaten,

On Thursday, Grace was led from judgment hall to judgment hall,

On Thursday, Grace was convicted by a fixed jury,

On Thursday, Grace was sentenced by Pilate,

On Friday, Grace was crucified on a cross,

On Friday, while hanging on a cross, Grace saved me and grace saved you,

With nails in His hands, Grace saved us.

With spikes in His feet, Grace saved us,

With a crown of thorns on His head, Grace saved us.

Grace looked beyond our half-hearted service.

Grace looked beyond out brokenness.

Grace looked beyond our backsliding.

Grace looked beyond our backbiting.

Grace looked beyond our unworthiness.

Grace looked beyond our faults and failures.

Grace looked beyond our sins and short comings.

Grace looked beyond our unfaithfulness.

Grace looked beyond our waywardness.

Grace looked beyond our wickedness.

You can call it good grace, hallelujah grace, healing grace, helping grace, redeeming grace, saving grace, soothing grace, thank you Jesus grace, or traveling grace, I choose to call it what my grandmother called it…simply Amazing grace.

"Amazing grace how sweet the sound that saved a wretch like me! I once was lost, but now I'm found, was blind but now I see.[7] Amazing grace shall always be my song of praise. For it was grace that brought my liberty; I do not know just why he came to love me, but I'm glad, I'm glad on today that Grace looked, beyond our faults and supplied all our need".[8]

Thank you Jesus... *It is Finished.*

The Seventh Word
(St. Luke 23:46)

"*And it was about the sixth hour (midday), and there was darkness over all the earth until the ninth hour (three o'clock). And the sun was darkened, and the veil of the temple was rent in the midst. And when Jesus had cried with a loud voice, he said; "Father, into thy hands I commend my spirit:" and having said thus, he gave up the ghost. Now when the centurion saw what was done, he glorified God, saying, certainly this was a righteous man. And all the people that came together to that sight, beholding the things which were done, smote their breasts, and returned. And all his acquaintance, and the women that followed him from Galilee, stood afar off, beholding these things*"* (Luke 23:44-49). The seventh saying of Christ on the cross unlike the sixth word is not a cry, nor was it a shout. It is best described as a soft tender prayer (St. Luke 23:44-49).

There was a great darkness as Jesus died. It was as if the sun itself could not bear to look upon the deed man's hands had done. The world is ever dark in the day when men seek to banish Christ. The Temple veil was torn in two. This was the veil which hid the Holy of Holies, the place where dwelt the very presence of God, the place where no man might ever enter except the High Priest, and he only once a year, on the great day of Atonement. It was as if the way to God's presence, previously barred to man, was thrown open for all of humanity to freely enter. It was as if the heart of God, previously hidden, was launched in clear view for the entire world to see. The birth, life and death of Jesus tore apart the veil, which some say, "separated God from man". "*He who has seen me,* "said Jesus, "*has seen the Father,*" (John 14:9) suddenly made sense. On the cross as never before, and perhaps never again, men saw the love of God.

Three of the Gospels tell us Jesus cried with a loud voice (Matthew 27:50; Luke 23:46; Mark 15:37.) The Gospel of John, on the other hand, does not mention this loud cry but tells us that Jesus died saying, "*It is finished*" (John 19:30). In the Greek and Aramaic languages the phrase "It is finished" is one word. It is finished and the great cry, are in fact, one and the same thing. Jesus died with a shout of triumph on his lips. He did not whisper the phrase, as one who is battered to his knees and forced to admit defeat. He shouted it like a victor who has won his last engagement with the enemy and brought a tremendous task to triumphant conclusion. *"It is Finished!"* was the cry of the Christ, crucified yet victorious.

The Sermon
The Hands of God

"Father, into thy hands I commend my spirit:" I'm reminded of a cute song I sang as a young boy every fourth Sunday; well, all of the young children at the church I attended would gather down front and together we would sing, "He's Got the Whole World in His Hands". The song went something like this,

"He's got the whole world in His hands."
"He's got the wind and the rain in His hands."
"He's got the tiny little baby in His hands."
"He's got you and me brother (sister) in His Hands."
"He's got the whole world in His hands."
Unknown Author

What better hands then the hands of God to be entrusted with the spirit of our Lord and our Christ. While dying on the cross Jesus prays ever so softly the first prayer that every Jewish boy and girl learns as a child, "*Into thy hand I commit my spirit: thou hast redeemed me, O Lord God of Truth.*" (Psalm 31:5). I'm reminded of a similar prayer that children in America prior to falling asleep have prayed since the eighteenth century:

> *Now I lay me down to sleep,*
> *I pray the Lord my soul to keep;*
> *And if I die before I wake,*
> *I pray the Lord my soul to take.*
>
> Unknown Author

This too is a prayer commending our soul into the loving and trusting hands of Elohim [God who is omnipresent and sovereign], Jehovah [The Lord of Promise], El-Shaddai [God almighty], Adonai [God Supreme Ruler], Jehovah-Jireh [God who will provide], Jehovah-Nissi [God my banner], Jehovah-Shalom [God my peace], Jehovah-Tsidkenu [God my righteousness], Jehovah-Rapheka [Lord who heals], Jehovah-Mekaddishkem [The Lord who sanctifies] and Elyon [The Most High God]. Whatever name we use He's still God.

As young children reciting this wonderful prayer, we didn't realize what we were truly praying and saying is, *"Father into thy hands I commend my spirit."* It was the hand of God that created the heaven and the earth. It was the hand of God that created the sun, moon and stars and place them high above the heavens. It was the hands of God that divided the waters (seas) from the dry land (earth). It was the hand of God that planted and brought forth grass, herb yielding seed and fruit trees yielding fruit. It was the hand of God which created and caused creatures to live in the waters (seas) and birds (fowl) to fly above the earth. It was the hand of God which created and caused living creatures, cattle, creeping things, and beast of all kind to inhabit the earth. Finally, it was the hands of God that created man.

As with my first book, I struggled with turning this manuscript over to the publishing company. Something in the back of my head, something within my spirit kept saying "not yet". It troubled me so that I finally begin praying to God specifically about a date to mail the manuscript to the publisher. I was delighted to finally hear God say, *"wait a little while longer, there's something I need for you to share with your readers.*" And so I began waiting. I waited until February 23, 2008 and God said add the following event to your book, and then mail your manuscript to the publisher.

In my first books I was led by the Holy Spirit to prayerfully share some very personal experiences. In the past I've written about real life situations which occurred in my own life or at a church located within the United States, however, the following didn't happen in a church, but rather at the world's largest Television & Media Company which is headquarter in the United States in New York and internationally in the Netherlands. It would be remised of me if I failed to say openly and honestly, it is not my intent to embarrass or cause any individual or group emotional pain or discomfort in writing about the following event. I truly believe Christians should teach, preach and write all God directs them to write. Furthermore, I hold to the belief the Word of God is meant to *comfort the disturbed and disturb the comfortable.*

I have a friend who is employed by the Television & Media Company located in Oldsmar, Florida. My friend has worked in the Information Technology field for years as a senior level programmer and/or manager. The Television &

Media Company annually conducts what is referred to as a PPR (employee evaluation) for all of its employees. In the time that my friends has been with the Television & Media Company her yearly performance reviews has resulted in a score of 3.0 out of 4.0 (fractional scoring isn't permitted so no employee could ever receive a .5 percentage rating. However, this year my friend was shocked to discover that she had been evaluated and received a score of 1.0 out 4.0. I spoke with my friend to see how she was feeling in an attempt to determine what her plan might be going forward, particularly since this comes at a time when the company is undergoing staff reductions. My friend is not the kind of person to walk away from a fight, particularly when she feels strongly that she's right. I wasn't at all surprised by what she shared with me because she is a very dynamic, spirit-filled Christian with a strong faith in God. My friend began by saying, "That she planned to remain employed in the Information Technology field and believes that God still has major work for her to complete while employed at the Television & Media Company. I then heard in her voice a renewed determination as she continue to say: "Apparently my manager needs to be reminded about the God of Israel, the God of Abraham, Isaac, and Jacob. Apparently he needs to be reminded of a few promises God has made to his children. *"For promotion comes neither from the East, nor from the West, nor from the South. But God is the judge; he puts down one, and lifts up another. All the strength of the wicked also will God cut off, but the strength of righteous shall be exalted"* (Psalm 75:6-7; 10).

"My brothers count if all joy when you fall into diver temptations (traps); knowing this, that the trying of your faith works patience. But let patience have her perfect work, that you may be perfect and complete wanting nothing." (James 1:2-4).*"Thou hast caused men to rule over our heads. We went through the fire and through the water: but thou (my God) brought us out to a wealthy place.* (Psalm 66:12).

By God's hands I was created. By God's hands I was delivered from the bondage of sin and the penalty of the second death. By God's hands I'll be vindicated. By God's hands this battle will be fought and won. By God's hands my enemies will become my foot stool. By God's hands the victory will be mine."

Brothers and sisters in Christ, there you have it, a powerful testimony from a powerful Christian about the powerful hands of God. No matter what issue, problem, challenge, lie or situation you are facing just remember God has you in his hands. Not some Television & Media Company, but the hands of God, continues to cloth and feed my friend and her co-workers. Not some Insurance Company, but the hands of God continue to replace and/or restore our losses. Not George H. W. Bush, the President, but the hands of God continues to cover and protect us. Not the military, but the hands of God continue to fight our battles. Not some doctor, but the hands of God, continues to heal our bodies. I'm glad that like my Lord Jesus I can boldly declare, *"Father, into thy hands I commend my spirit"*. I pray the Lord you can too.

- You came out of the night club by the hand of God.
- You were delivered from drug addiction by the hand of God.
- You were kept from becoming HIV infected by the hand of God.
- Your life was spared in spite of the heart attack by the head of God.
- Your life was spared in spite of the stroke by the hand of God.
- Your life was spared in spite of being shot by the hand of God.
- You got the job by the hand of God.
- You got the promotion by the hand of God.

- You'll keep your job by the hand of God.
- Your peace came by the hand of God.
- Enoch was taken up so that he would not see death by hand of God.
- Noah being warned by God about things not yet seen, in reverence prepared an ark for the salvation of his family and was saved by the hand of God.
- Sarah's ability to conceive a man-child came by the hand of God.
- The three Old Testament Hebrew boys were kept safe by the hands of God.
- Rev. Dr. Martin Luther King's dream of one America is coming true by the hands of God.
- Senator Barak Obama may be elected the first Black President or Senator Hillary Clinton may be elected as the first woman President of the United States by the hand of God.
- Racism will be destroyed by the hands of God.
- Supervisors and Managers at companies who foolishly misrepresent facts will be disciplined by the hand of God.

I'm still reminded of that cute song that I sang as a child, "He's Got the Whole World in His Hands", but as an adult, with adult challenges, struggles and problems, I've learned and sang a new song entitled, "Hold to God's Unchanging Hand".

"Time is filled with swift transition, Naught of earth unmoved can stand,
Build your hopes on things eternal, Hold to God's unchanging hand!
Hold to God's unchanging hand! Hold to God's unchanging hand!
Trust in Him who will not leave you, Whatsoever, years may bring;
If by earthly friends forsaken, Still more closely to Him cling!
Hold to God's unchanging hand! Hold to God's unchanging hand!
Covet not this world's vain riches, That so rapidly decay;
Seek to gain the heavenly treasures, They will never pass away!
Hold to God's unchanging hand! Hold to God's unchanging hand!
When your journey is completed, If to God you have been true,
Fair and bright the home in glory, Your enraptured soul will view!
Hold to God's unchanging hand! Hold to God's unchanging hand!
Build your hopes on things eternal, Hold to God's unchanging hand!"

"Father into your hands I commend my Spirit."

The Seventh Word
Another Look (St. Luke 23:46)

I recently received word that one of my spiritual sons in ministry, Rev. Christopher Paul would be traveling back to Tampa from North Carolina to preach one of the seven last sayings at Beulah Baptist Church during the six thirty evening service. Chris is a first year graduate student at Shaw Divinity School working toward completion of a Master of Divinity degree. Upon hearing the news I called Chris to confirm the news. During our conversation I informed Chris that I had completed this book and mailed the manuscript to the PublishAmerica several weeks before and was looking forward to the release of the book. Chris shared with me that he had been assigned to preach on this seventh saying, *"Father, into thy hands I commend my spirit".* Looking back on the conversation I recall suggesting to Chris that if he so desired I would send him a copy of the sermon I wrote entitled, *"The Hands of God"* which I thought would assist him in preparing for his March 21st 2008 preachment. Well, to no one's surprise Chris preached a powerful message. The next morning I emailed Chris the following:

"Preacher thank, you for allowing God to speak through you on last night. Your delivery was awesome. What a dynamic Word. Continue to stay grounded and rooted in the Word of Christ and never take your eyes off of the true prize. Pastor Favorite is correct continue your education and walk with integrity, for God will take you to higher heights. There were several points you made during your preachment and with your permission I will attempt to incorporate the key ideas into my book provided, and of course I will give you credit".

Well, Chris I considered the idea of adding excerpts of your message to this book; however, God spoke and said no…add Chris's complete sermon to this book. It is an honor my son for me to share with others what God shared through you, what I call another look at the seventh saying of Jesus Christ on the Cross.

The Sermon
"The Hands of God"
Rev. Chris Paul

A few years ago a national insurance company came up
with a very catchy slogan. Adults knew it. Young adults
knew it. Children knew it. It simply said, *"You're in good hands
with Allstate."* The commercials consisted of a seemingly
happy family with the announcer recounting some tragic
story that had taken place in their life. The images that are
planted in the mind are that if a time of tragedy ever comes
in your own life you can count on Allstate Insurance
Company to be there for you and your family.

The suggestion that Allstate was attempting to make is
that in those times when life is not favorable—when there is

REVEREND DR. VINCENT P. TAYLOR

physical pain, financial loss, loss of health, and devaluation of stock portfolio, or perhaps a car accident, you don't have to fear or worry because Allstate Insurance is there for you.

It sounds good and it's wonderful to know that if you are involved in an automobile accident you're in good hands with Allstate. It sounds marvelous and reassuring to know that if a spouse should suddenly die and you don't know how you're going to make ends meet, you're in good hands with Allstate. It sounds encouraging and edifying to know that if your house is destroyed due to wind, hurricane, fire or a flood, you're in good hands with Allstate. It's comforting to know that should your Suzuki GSXR be stolen, and your rims are ripped off, that you're in good hands with Allstate.

I've come today to suggest that if you're looking to Allstate or State Farm or any other insurance company to meet your needs, you may be sadly mistaken...amen hurricane Katrina. There are some things in this life that no amount of insurance can truly replace. There is no insurance for a broken heart. There is no insurance for the storms of divorce. There is no insurance for a child that was raised right and decides to use drugs anyway. There is no insurance for having your name scandalized. There is no insurance for your steps moving slower (growing old). There is no insurance for a life affected by HIV and AIDS. There is no insurance for tossing and turning while attempting to fall asleep at night. There is no insurance for worrying about what tomorrow will bring. But I've come to tell you on this Good Friday night of a better insurance offered through a blessed assurance, called the *hands of God.*

Here in this text, we find the author Luke vividly describing the physical atmosphere of the time in which our Savior died. Luke records that it was about 12 noon, yet there was darkness over the entire earth until about 3pm. Even this earth, God's initial creation alongside the Heavens, showed sorrow and cringed from every drop of blood that fell from Jesus' battered body onto its soil. Even the sun in all its radiance and brilliance, hid its face being unable to bear witness to this tragic moment.

The world is ever dark in the day which men seek to banish Christ. Sadly, much hasn't changed we're living in a day in which men still seek to banish Christ and sadly it has even infected our churches. The question which begs to be asked is how can one be in church, yet seek to banish Christ? I'm glad you asked. I turn on what's ironically called The Word Network and see a bunch of jokers in shiny suits that always fail to preach the Cross and Him crucified, but they never fail to tell me that my blessing is on the way. They never fail to tell us that God's going to do it. These so call Prophets prophesy through the television screen telling us to call the 800 number at the bottom of our television sets to get our very own supply of some miracle spring water because it will end our financial woes. They tell us to believe it and receive it; to name it and claim it. God is not a genie in a bottle. You can name and claim, that E-Class all you want. You can go to the dealership, walk around the car seven times and shout all you want, but if you don't have the money, you aren't getting that car. And it's a pitch black darkened day in the body of Christ when we equate blessings to material things. But the true blessings of the Kingdom are intangible.

We are blessed to be abiding in God's grace. We're blessed that God hasn't seen fit to destroy us in spite of our wickedness. We're blessed because Jesus commended His Spirit into the hands of God, presenting us faultless before God's throne of grace. But just because Jesus has commended His Spirit into God's hands, and we've received God's grace because of it, it doesn't mean that righteousness and holiness get thrown out the window. Preachers get pressured to preach this watered down gospel because somebody might get offended, somebody might get convicted, and take their tithe and go home. Well the Word of God ought to convict you! There's something wrong if you sit in church Sunday after Sunday and nothing said across the pulpit ever knocks you off of your pivot. The word of God comes to make us better. Proverbs says that iron sharpens iron and sometimes the sparks may have to fly to get us back on track to where God would have us to be.

But thank God that the Temple veil was torn in two. This was the veil which hid the place where the presence of God dwelt, the place where no man other than the High Priest dared entered, and he entered only once a year, on the great day of Atonement. It was as if the way to God's presence, previously barred to man, was thrown open for all of humanity to freely enter. It was as if the heart of God, previously hidden, was launched in clear view for the entire world to see. Jesus, the Fulfillment of the Law and the Prophets, chooses as His last words, the phrase that He let his father, David, borrow back in Psalm 31:5—*"Father, into thy hands I commend my Spirit"*. Christ commended or deposited His life back into His Father's hands. What does that signify? And how does it apply to us? Jesus' choice last words signified him relinquishing His life into God's control. In everything Jesus did, He set an example for His disciples to follow. So yes, Jesus commended His spirit as a part of His purpose and role in our salvation, but I also argue that He commended His Spirit into God's hands as an example for us to take heed to. We too are to lay down our will, and deposit our lives in to the hands of God. But how often do we find ourselves in the wrong hands? How often do we find ourselves trusting in the wrong things or the wrong people? We relentlessly search on an unending quest for knowledge to help sustain ourselves and all we have to do is deposit our lives into the Master's hands. Oh! If we could have that mindset. If we would only deposit our entire being, back into the Master's hands, if we would only give Christ our all. But there's just something about us in which we want to be in control. We struggle with laying down our will. We are anxious about letting God take the wheel in our journey through life.

But if we can ever come to the understanding of whose hands we're in. Just think about the following: A basketball in my hands is worth about nineteen dollars. A basketball in Michael Jordan's hands is worth over thirty three million dollars. It depends whose hands it's in. A football in my hands is worth about six dollars. A football in one of the

Payton brother's hands will get you back to back NFL Super Bowl championships, plus million of dollars. It depends on whose hands it's in. A tennis racket is useless in my hands. A tennis racket in Serena Williams' hands is worth millions of dollars. It depends on whose hands it's in. A rod in my hands will keep away an angry dog or beat your kids if they get out of line. A rod in Moses' hands will part the mighty sea. It depends whose hands it's in. A slingshot in my hands is a kid's toy. A slingshot in David's hand causes giants to fall. It depends whose hands it's in. Two fish and five loaves of bread in my hands is a couple of fish sandwiches. Two fish and five loaves of bread in Jesus' hands will feed five thousand men, their five thousand wives, and their five thousand children....so at least fifteen thousand people....or as the Bible put it, the multitudes! It depends whose hands it's in. Nails in my hands might produce a stack of shelves. Nails in Jesus Christ's hands will produce salvation for the entire world. And I can guarantee you that no matter your sins it's been nailed to the cross! It depends whose hands it's in.

Your soul in your hand is worthless, and doomed for damnation. But your soul in God's hands causes your name to be written in the Lamb's Book of Life, in addition to abundant life while we're passing through on earth. It depends on whose hands it's in. So put your concerns, your worries, your fears, your hopes, your dreams, your families and your relationships in God's hands because our God is able to do exceedingly abundantly above all that we can ask or think according to the power that works in us.

My prayer is that we will all leave here tonight, saying Father I deposit my life into your hands. Have your way with me. Use me to your glory. May God bless us all as we draw closer to Him.

Conclusion
Final Reflection

The Apostle Paul writes the following about our calling and about our spiritual battle: *"For the weapons of our warfare are not carnal but mighty in God for pulling down strongholds, casting down arguments and every high thing that exalts itself against the knowledge of God, bringing every thought into captivity to the obedience of Christ"* (II Corinthians 10:5).

It is the calling and responsibility of every believer and follower of Jesus Christ to learn how to bring every thought into the obedience of Christ. When we find ourselves in physical or emotional pains, stressed out or spiritually embattled, and our emotions scattered all over the place, it's very easy to simply react anyway we feel like to circumstances which surround us, and not be willing to discipline our reactions in a godly way. Our conscience may even prod us to react better but there are times when we just don't care and decide to do as we please. We react in the heat of the moment.

When our pain and stress levels are low it's much easier to live God's way. The real test comes when our pain and our stress levels are high. In times like these it's wise to remember the ultimate example of how to react during such times of pain and stress. Jesus Christ's example on the cross provides great inspiration and teachings to encourage Christians and non-Christians to control our thoughts and to think through our reactions to great emotional and physical pain. Several viewers of the controversial Mel Gibson movie "The Passion of the Christ" commented, "After seeing the full enormity of what Christ went through that their respect and admiration for Christ's discipline to react to all of that in such a godly way went through the roof".

The seven last sayings of Jesus Christ on the Cross reveal Jesus' innermost feelings as He poured out His life for us and provide a powerful example of how we, too, should react in times of great physical and emotional pain.

The First Word: *"But Jesus was saying, Father, forgive them, for they do not know what they are doing"* (Luke 23:34). Instead of being consumed with his own pain and misery, Jesus asked forgiveness for those responsible for the evil done to Him and by extension, all who continue to allow themselves to be controlled and ruled by sin. The question which begs to be asked is what did Christ mean when He said *"for they do not know what they do"*? These hardened Roman soldiers didn't crucify Christ accidentally so what did He mean that they didn't know what they were doing?

Perhaps, the following Scriptures provides a clue or suggestions, for it says *"Jesus, the author and finisher of our faith, who for the joy that was set before Him endured the cross"* (Hebrews 12:2). It says Jesus' mind was totally fixed on the joy that was set before Him. It was the burning vision of victory for mankind He was about to complete and His coming Kingdom that kept Him going at this time.

It is also this vision that helps us to understand what Christ meant when He said that they did not know what they were doing? Jesus may have projected His mind forward to the time when these soldiers will be resurrected and the full magnitude of their role in his death will hit them. When we are deeply hurt by others, I believe it will aid us if we also

115

have this kind of vision and project our mind forward to when those who hurt us will come to their senses and repent of their actions. It also helps to remember that everyone is a potential son or daughter of God.

The Second Word: *"And He said to him, Truly, I say to you, today you will be with me in Paradise"* (Luke 23:43). The two thieves who were crucified with Christ, had early on joined bystanders in mocking Jesus (Mark 15:32). The Gospel of Luke tells us in Luke 24:39, *"One of the criminals who hung there hurled insults at him: 'Aren't you the Christ? Save yourself and us!'"* It's very clear, that this malefactor (thief) wanted only escape from his pain. This criminal had no desire to know Jesus as his personal Lord and Saviour and to repent of his sins but a miraculous change occurred in the other criminal. He was convinced through the words spoken to him by Jesus to believe. He, too, had mocked Jesus earlier, but now he rebuked the other criminal.

We are not told of any other conversation between this second criminal and Jesus. Perhaps only Jesus' example and prayer, which he overheard, moved him deeply. He said, *"Lord, remember me when you come into your kingdom"* (Luke 23:42). Jesus replied by offering him hope for the future: *"I tell you the truth today you will be with me in paradise"* (Luke 23:43).

By paradise did Christ mean that this criminal would go straight to heaven? Now, we know that wasn't the case. What Jesus did know was that in the moment after this criminal's legs were broken and he died that he would come up in presumably the second resurrection which would seem like the same day to him. At that time the earth would have been transformed into a paradise and he will have his chance to receive salvation.

Again we see the incredible vision that He had on the cross. He just kept focusing ahead on the "joy that was set before Him" as it says in Hebrews 12:2. This kind of vision, this kind of thinking way ahead to the end result can help us to keep things in perspective and to encourage others when we, too, are suffering and it can help us to temper our responses in a godly way.

The Third Word: *"When Jesus then saw His mother, and the disciple whom He loved standing nearby, He said to His mother, "Woman, behold, your son!" Then He said to the disciple, "Behold your, mother!" From that hour the disciple took her into his own household."* (John 19:26-27).

Jesus' mother Mary had four other sons—James, Joses, Simon and Judas. One would think that one of them would physically care for Mary. John 7:5 says that during His ministry Jesus' brothers did not believe in Him. Paul notes in 1 Corinthians 15:7 that He appeared to His brother James after His resurrection and this is probably when he and his brothers began to believe as they are with Mary and the apostles in Acts 1:14 when a replacement is chosen for Judas. James became the leader of the Jerusalem church while Judas or Jude later wrote the epistle of Jude. What need of Mary did Jesus perceive on the cross that wasn't being met here by His brothers? That John took Mary into his home implies a physical need. Whether it was a physical or perhaps a spiritual need that wasn't being met, Jesus saw to it that His disciple John would take care of His mother. Again, instead of being consumed with his own pain and misery, Jesus cared for those around Him. Over the years, I've been privileged to visit hundred of sick people in their homes, hospitals and nursing homes. I truly cherish the visits with those who have blessed me far more than I blessed them. For you see, even in pain, sickness, and facing death many were at peace. At no time did they ever take their eyes or their hope off of Jesus. At no time did their faith ever weaken. At no time did doubt ever cross their mind that one day they would recover from their sickness or should death be their fate that they wouldn't see King Jesus face-to-face.

The Fourth Word: *"And about the ninth hour Jesus cried with a loud voice, saying, "Eli, Eli, la ma sabach thani?" that is "My God, My God, why have you forsaken me?"* (Matthew 27:46; Mark 15:34). The Apostle Paul perhaps referred to this moment when he wrote in 2 Corinthians 5:21: *"For He made Him who knew no sin to be sin for us, that we might become the righteousness of God in Him."* At this moment the Father placed on Him the sins of humanity to be paid as He was about to die. Isaiah 59:2 states that our sins separate us from God. During his entire adult life, Jesus had an intimate and vibrant relationship with God as His Father. Suddenly, while suffering the agony and fatigue of crucifixion, Jesus could no longer feel that wonderful heavenly presence. At this moment He could empathize with all of us when we feel separated from God because of our sins and guilt.

The Fifth Word: *"After this, Jesus knowing that all things were now accomplished, that the Scripture might be fulfilled, saith, I thirst."* (John 19:28). The time of final sacrifice was close. Jesus had endured and overcome the heat, pain, rejection and loneliness. He could have suffered and died in silence. Instead, unexpectedly, it appears that he asked for help. "Knowing that all was now complete, and so that the

Scripture would be fulfilled, Jesus said, "*I thirst*" (John 19:28).

Earlier He'd been offered the same drink but with added gall. He refused it as recorded in Matthew 27:34. Why refuse it earlier and now take a drink at the moment of death? There are several conservative commentaries, which makes this comment about the vinegar mixed with gall: The narcotic drink would have helped deaden the pain, but Jesus refused it. He drank the cup of suffering instead. Instead of reaching for a comforter, He was prepared to take the difficult but necessary path. When finally He had fully drank of the cup of suffering Jesus then appears to ask for a drink. I suppose one of many lessons for us to learn from this saying is to learn how to take the high road when it's necessary rather than the low road.

The Sixth Word: "*When Jesus therefore had received the vinegar, he said. It is finished: and he bowed his head, and gave up the ghost.*" (John 19:30). The sixth saying of Christ on the cross is one of triumph. John 19:30 says: "*When he had received the drink, Jesus said, 'It is finished.' With that, He bowed His head and gave up his spirit*".

Jesus' humility rings in his words. His was not a vain, I-showed-you attitude. He did not even say, "I did it" or "I did it my way" as Frank Sinatra used to sing. He claimed no credit. To the end, Jesus' mind was on the work He came to do. He triumphantly announced, for all to hear, "It is finished."

The Seventh Word: *"Father, into your hands I commend my spirit"* (Luke 23:46). When he had said this, He breathed his last. He looked forward to finally being fully reunited with His Father. At that dramatic moment Jesus died for you and me and became the true Passover sacrifice for each and every one of us. The way that John records his gospel, at first, gives the impression that Jesus died first before the soldier thrust his spear into Jesus' side which is how it is portrayed in "The Passion of the Christ". In "The Passion" the soldiers suspect He is already dead and one of them thrusts him in the side to test that He is dead.

The original text of Matthew's gospel helps clear up the confusion of whether He died before or after the spear was thrust into Him. In Matthew 27:49, after He took the drink of vinegar, we read, *"But the rest said, 'Let Him alone! Let us see if Elijah comes to save Him.'"* Most Bible versions then go straight to verse 50 which says that He cried out again and gave up His spirit.

Fred Coulter in his "A Harmony of the Gospels" writes,

"The latter half of this verse, which begins with the words 'Then another took a spear...' has been omitted from the King James Version. However, a majority of ancient manuscripts contain this part of the verse; these manuscripts include the codex Vaticanus and Sinaiticus. Older translations which contain the complete verse are the Moffatt translation and the Fenton translation" (p. 304). From the latter half of verse 49 it should read, *"Then another took a spear and thrust it into His side and out came water and blood. And after crying out again with a loud voice, Jesus yielded up His spirit."*

In summation, it is a tough calling to bring every thought into the obedience of Christ, especially when we are in great pain physically and emotionally. As we study the perfect caring example of Christ as He suffered on the cross leading up to the Passover season, it should be a great motivation to all of us to live and to react in a godly way at all times, both good and bad.

Bibliography

Wikipedia, Encyclopedia

Hauerwas, Stanley. Meditations on the Seven Last Words: Cross-Shattered Christ. Grand Rapids: Brazon Press, 2004

Rutledge, Fleming. The Seven Last Words from the Cross. Wm. B. Eerdmans Publishing, 2005

Neuhaus, Richard. Death on a Friday Afternoon. New York, NY: Basic Books, 2000

The New National Baptist Hymnal. Nashville: National Baptist Publishing Board, 1977

Book Reviews

"In this book Rev. Vincent P. Taylor does an outstanding job in his exegesis and application of the text. He finds himself in the text and shares with his audience from the reservoir of his heart. It's always refreshing when preachers wrestle with some of the less familiar, yet rich text of the Word."

Darrell E. Wilson
Senior Minister
New Beginnings Christian Church
Louisville, Kentucky

"An extremely well-documented book, the Dr. Vincent Taylor addresses the historical and spiritual, significances of the seven last

saying of our Lord, uttered from the Cross. Dr. Taylor makes a bold and daring attempt to show the relevance of the seven last saying to the Christian Church. From the beginning chapter "The First Word: A Lesson on Forgiveness from the Kings of Kings," to the ending chapter "The Seventh Word: The Hands of God" readers will be drawn through the pages by Dr. Taylor's easy-going style that allows one to leap from the concept on the page into life-changing understanding of what our Lord endured on our behalf, but more importantly the riches He left for us in the seven last sayings. Rarely, will you read such religious, power packed into so few pages

"Each chapter offers, fresh new insight into the seven last saying of Jesus on the Cross. Sectioned into manageable chapters with an easy-to-read instruction, couples with great sermon writing, blended with great story telling, this book is a must read.

"I believe this work, will challenge readers to pursue God in worship and love as a part of everyday life. In addition I believe this work will redefine and reshape the views many Christian have regarding Good Friday; as well as, Easter in a positive manner."

Deacon William Pinkston, III
Deputy Director of News Technology
The Atlanta Journal-Constitution
Atlanta, GA

Endnotes

[1] Wm B. Eerdmans Publishing
[2] Death on a Friday Afternoon
[3] Wikipedia, Encyclopedia
[4] Wikipedia, Encyclopedia
[5] Wikipedia, Encyclopedia
[6] Wikipedia, Encyclopedia
[7] The New National Baptist Hymnal
[8] The New National Baptist Hymnal
[9] The New National Baptist Hymnal

Also by Vincent P. Taylor

When a Nobody
Becomes Somebody
by Vincent P. Taylor

"This "riveting" resource is a must-have for those seeking a
better understanding of God and the importance of
maintaining a relationship with Him..."
- LONNIE JOHNSON, SENIOR MINISTER